TRUTH

Abolitionist and Activist

W9-AYP-639

Charlotte Taylor

E | **Enslow Publishing**
101 W. 23rd Street
Suite 240
New York, NY 10011
USA
enslow.com

Words to Know

abolitionist—Someone who works to end slavery.

autobiography—The story of a person's life written by that person.

commune—A community in which everyone shares similar ideas and is treated fairly.

harvest—To gather a season's crops.

inspire—To fill with excitement about something.

petition—A formal way to ask for something to be done.

preach—To give talks about God.

reformer—Someone who works to change or improve society.

right—Something that everyone should be able to have or do.

sojourn—A brief stay or visit.

sue—To take someone to court.

Union—The name for the North in the US Civil War.

Contents

Sojourner Truth

CHAPTER 1

Slave Girl

Sojourner Truth was the daughter of slaves who lived in Ulster County, New York. When she was born in 1797, her parents named her Isabella. Isabella's father was James Bomefree and her mother's name was Betsey. Johannes Hardenbergh owned the family. He was a rich Dutch man who had a great deal of land. Isabella and her family spoke Dutch.

Isabella was the youngest of twelve children. Her brothers and sisters were sold or given away before she was born. Isabella knew only one of her brothers, Peter. She knew that her parents were very sad about

This house belonged to Johannes Hardenbergh, Isabella's first owner.

the loss of their other children. This sad feeling stayed with Isabella, too.

Isabella Is Sold

In 1808 Isabella was taken from her parents. She was sold to an English-speaking owner. She was sold several more times in her early life. From 1810 to 1827, she worked for John J. Dumont of New Paltz, New York.

Isabella planted, plowed, and **harvested** crops. She also milked cows. In the house, she sewed, cooked, and cleaned. During this time, Sojourner married another slave named Thomas in 1815. Together they had three children.

Dumont told Isabella she could go free in 1826. Later she hurt her hand. She was unable to work as hard as usual. Dumont felt he was cheated. He broke his promise. Isabella left with her baby anyway. Isabella later learned that Dumont had illegally sold her son, Peter. With the help of friends she **sued** Dumont. Peter was freed in 1828.

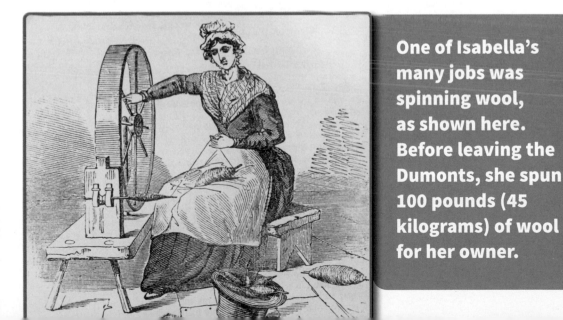

One of Isabella's many jobs was spinning wool, as shown here. Before leaving the Dumonts, she spun 100 pounds (45 kilograms) of wool for her owner.

Sojourner Says:

"It is the mind that makes the body."

Isabella's family members may have been sold at slave auctions like this one. Often families were broken up and sold to different owners.

CHAPTER 2

Isabella's New Life

After Isabella escaped from Dumont in 1826, she needed a place to live. A friend knew some people who could help her. Isaac and Maria Van Wagener lived just a few miles down the road. They took in Isabella for the rest of her time as a slave. The Van Wageners did not believe in slavery. Isabella and her baby, Sophia, lived with them for a year.

In 1827 Isabella went to an African Dutch slave holiday celebration called Pinkster. There she had a powerful religious experience. Religion became an important part of her life from then on.

For the rest of her life, Isabella would hear voices and see visions. Her spirituality helped keep her strong and brave.

Runaway slaves had to be very careful. Slave catchers were paid to track them down and return them to their owners, who would punish them.

Isabella Preaches

Around 1829, Isabella moved to New York City. She took her two youngest children, Peter and Sophia, with her. Isabella met a wealthy social **reformer** named Elijah Pierson. She joined him in **preaching** in the streets.

Isabella could not read, but she was a very good speaker. She became well known for her preaching, praying, and singing.

Sojourner Says:

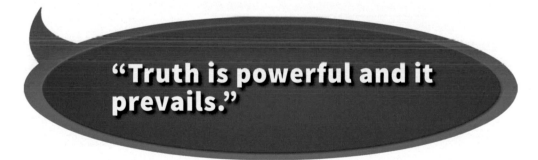

"Truth is powerful and it prevails."

Isabella and her children moved to New York. The city was crowded with people. Isabella would stand in the street and preach to anyone who would listen.

CHAPTER 3
Speaking God's Truth

Isabella loved to preach. She decided that she would become a traveling preacher. Isabella said that voices told her to **sojourn** the Northeast and Midwest. To sojourn means to make short visits. In 1843 she began to go around the country, speaking God's truth. Isabella changed her name to Sojourner Truth. From then on, she thought of June 1, 1843, as her birthday.

In the winter of 1844, Sojourner Truth moved to a **commune** in Massachusetts. It was called the Northampton Association for Education and Industry.

There she met other members of the **abolitionist** (antislavery) movement. Abolitionism and women's **rights** became important to Sojourner Truth. She began to preach about these ideas, too.

Sojourner's Story

In 1850 Sojourner published her **autobiography**. It was called *The Narrative of Sojourner Truth*. She

Sojourner never learned to read or write properly. But when she preached, her words inspired people from all different backgrounds.

In the middle of the 1800s, the antislavery movement started to grow stronger. Here abolitionist Wendell Phillips speaks to a crowd about the evils of slavery.

sold it at women's rights meetings for 25 cents per copy. In 1851 she gave a speech in Ohio at the Akron Women's Rights Convention. She talked about being a slave. She talked about the sadness of having her own children sold.

Sojourner Says:

"If women want any rights more than they's got, why don't they just take them, and not be talking about it."

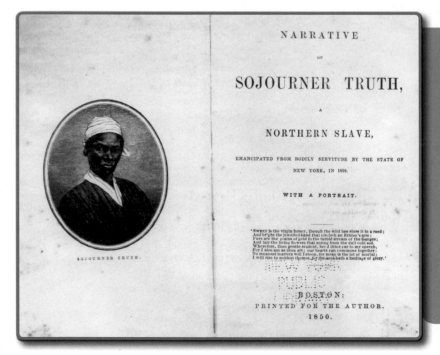

Since Sojourner could not write, she told her life story to her friend, who wrote it down for her. It was published by abolitionist William Lloyd Garrison.

CHAPTER 4

The Fight for Rights

Many slaves had a hard time starting a new life after they were freed. Sojourner wanted to help them. In the mid-1850s, she moved to Battle Creek, Michigan. This was an important place for the antislavery movement. She helped freed slaves find jobs. She helped Michigan's black army soldiers. She also worked to allow blacks to travel with whites on streetcars in Washington, DC.

When the Civil War began in 1861, Sojourner wanted to help the black soldiers who were fighting for the North. She raised money for the troops by giving speeches and singing. Sojourner also helped black soldiers join the **Union** army.

A Full Life

In 1864 Sojourner met with President Abraham Lincoln at the White House. In 1870 Sojourner sent a **petition** to Congress. In it she asked the government

Sojourner wanted to help the Union win the Civil War. She helped black men join the army.

Sojourner Truth and President Abraham Lincoln both helped to free the slaves. Here the president shows Sojourner a Bible that was given to him by a group of black people from Maryland.

Sojourner Says:

"I am not going to die, I'm going home like a shooting star."

to give land in the West to former slaves. Congress did not do anything for former slaves. Sojourner **inspired** thousands of former slaves to settle their homes in Kansas.

Sojourner continued to travel and speak in the 1870s. She talked about a homeland for blacks in the West. She gave speeches about equal rights for women and blacks. She died on November 26, 1883. In 1986 Sojourner Truth was honored on a US postage stamp.

Sojourner Truth
22
Black Heritage USA

Sojourner was honored in 1986 with a US postage stamp. Over a hundred years after her death, people still remember her as a voice that spoke for equal rights for all people.

Timeline

1797—Isabella is born into slavery in Ulster County, New York.

1815—Isabella marries another slave, Thomas.

1808—Isabella is taken from her parents and sold to another owner.

1826—Isabella escapes to freedom with her infant daughter, Sophia.

1827—New York State abolishes slavery.

1827—Isabella goes to a Pinkster celebration.

1828—Isabella wins a lawsuit to free her son, Peter, who had been illegally sold into slavery by Dumont.

1829—Isabella moves to New York City with her son, Peter, and daughter Sophia.

1843—At age forty-six, Isabella adopts the name Sojourner Truth.

1850—Sojourner Truth publishes her autobiography.

1856—Sojourner moves to Battle Creek, Michigan.

1870—Sojourner sends a petition to Congress asking the government for a black homeland.

1883—Sojourner Truth dies in Battle Creek, Michigan, on November 26.

Learn More

Books

Evans, Shane W. *Underground: Finding the Light to Freedom.* New York: Square Fish, 2015.

Mara, Wil. *Abraham Lincoln*. New York: Scholastic, 2014.

Turner, Ann. *My Name Is Truth: The Life of Sojourner Truth*. New York: HarperCollins, 2015.

Websites

www.sojournertruth.org/History/Biography
Includes detailed information about the life and legacy of Sojourner Truth.

www.ducksters.com/history/civil_rights/sojourner_ truth.php
Provides a brief biography of Sojourner Truth plus facts and links to related sites.

Index

Published in 2016 by Enslow Publishing, LLC.
101 W. 23rd Street, Suite 240, New York, NY 10011

Copyright © 2016 by Enslow Publishing, LLC.

All rights reserved.

No part of this book may be reproduced by any means without the written permission of the publisher.

Library of Congress Cataloging-in-Publication Data
Taylor, Charlotte, 1978- author.
 Sojourner Truth : abolitionist and activist / Charlotte Taylor.
    pages cm. — (Exceptional African Americans)
 Includes bibliographical references and index.
 Summary: "Describes the life, work, and contributions of activist Sojourner Truth before and during the American Civil War"—Provided by publisher.
 Audience: Ages 8 and up.
 ISBN 978-0-7660-7372-2 (library binding)
 ISBN 978-0-7660-7370-8 (pbk.)
 ISBN 978-0-7660-7371-5 (6-pack)
1. Truth, Sojourner, 1799-1883—Juvenile literature. 2. African American abolitionists—Biography—Juvenile literature.
3. Abolitionists—United States—Biography—Juvenile literature.
4. Social reformers—United States—Biography—Juvenile literature. I. Title.
 E185.97.T8T36 2016
 326'.8092—dc23
 [B]
                      2015026938

Printed in the United States of America

To Our Readers: We have done our best to make sure all website addresses in this book were active and appropriate when we went to press. However, the author and the publisher have no control over and assume no liability for the material available on those websites or on any websites they may link to. Any comments or suggestions can be sent by e-mail to customerservice@enslow.com.

Photo Credits: Throughout book, © Toria/Shutterstock.com (blue background); cover, pp. 1, 14 Time Life Pictures/Timepix/The LIFE Picture Collection/Getty Images; pp. 4, 7 Hulton Archive/Getty Images; p. 6 Ralph Le Fevre/State University of New York at New Paltz/Wikimedia Commons/1903 HardenberghHouseBk.jpg/public domain; p. 8 The Print Collector/Print Collector/Hulton Archive/Getty Images; pp. 10, 15 © North Wind Archives; p. 12 Prisma/UIG/Getty Images; p. 16 MPI/Archive Photos/Getty Images; p. 18 Kean Collection/Archive Photos/Getty Images; p. 19 Library of Congress, Prints and Photographs Division; p. 21 Netfali/Shutterstock.com.